# Experience Marketing: Concepts, Frameworks and Consumer Insights

**Bernd Schmitt**

*Columbia Business School*
*Columbia University*
*New York, NY 10027*
*USA*
*bhs1@columbia.edu*

## now

**the essence of knowledge**

Boston – Delft

# Foundations and Trends® in Marketing

*Published, sold and distributed by:*
now Publishers Inc.
PO Box 1024
Hanover, MA 02339
USA
Tel. +1-781-985-4510
www.nowpublishers.com
sales@nowpublishers.com


*Outside North America:*
now Publishers Inc.
PO Box 179
2600 AD Delft
The Netherlands
Tel. +31-6-51115274


The preferred citation for this publication is B. Schmitt, Experience Marketing: Concepts, Frameworks and Consumer Insights, Foundations and Trends® in Marketing, vol 5, no 2, pp 55–112, 2010


ISBN: 978-1-60198-452-4
© 2011 B. Schmitt

# Foundations and Trends® in Marketing
## Volume 5 Issue 2, 2010
## Editorial Board

# Editorial Scope

**Foundations and Trends® in Marketing** will publish survey and tutorial articles in the following topics:

- B2B Marketing
- Bayesian Models
- Behavioral Decision Making
- Branding and Brand Equity
- Channel Management
- Choice Modeling
- Comparative Market Structure
- Competitive Marketing Strategy
- Conjoint Analysis
- Customer Equity
- Customer Relationship Management
- Game Theoretic Models
- Group Choice and Negotiation
- Discrete Choice Models
- Individual Decision Making

- Marketing Decisions Models
- Market Forecasting
- Marketing Information Systems
- Market Response Models
- Market Segmentation
- Market Share Analysis
- Multi-channel Marketing
- New Product Diffusion
- Pricing Models
- Product Development
- Product Innovation
- Sales Forecasting
- Sales Force Management
- Sales Promotion
- Services Marketing
- Stochastic Model

## Information for Librarians

Foundations and Trends® in Marketing, 2010, Volume 5, 4 issues. ISSN paper version 1555-0753. ISSN online version 1555-0761. Also available as a combined paper and online subscription.

Foundations and Trends® in
Marketing
Vol. 5, No. 2 (2010) 55–112
© 2011 B. Schmitt
DOI: 10.1561/1700000027

now
the essence of knowledge

# Experience Marketing: Concepts, Frameworks and Consumer Insights

## Bernd Schmitt

*Columbia Business School, Columbia University, New York, NY 10027, USA, bhs1@columbia.edu*

## Abstract

Experience is a new and exciting concept marketing academia and practice. This monograph reviews the various meanings of experience as the term is used in philosophy, psychology, and in consumer behavior and marketing. I will discuss the key concepts of experience marketing such as experiential value, different types of experiences, the distinction between ordinary and extraordinary experiences and experience touchpoints. I will also review the empirical findings that provide consumer insights on experiences — such as how experiences are remembered, whether positive and negative experiences can co-exist, how experiential attributes are processed and whether experiences are rational. Practical frameworks for managing and marketing experiences will be discussed. I will conclude with an exploration of how experience marketing can contribute to customer happiness.

# Contents

# 1

## Introduction

Consider some of the intriguing new products and brands that have appeared on the market during the first decade of the 21st century: Apple with its iPod, iPhone and iPad products, Nintendo's Wii and Vitamin Water, just to name a few. All these products boast innovative designs and promise superior function. But focusing on their product features tells only a part of the story. Just as creative and innovative is the way these brands are marketed to consumers — through appeals to our senses, feelings, intellect, curiosity, and self-image rather than to more rational, utilitarian notions of value. Such marketing techniques have turned up in all sorts of industries, from consumer electronics and automotives, to airlines and retailing. Think of the Mini Cooper, Jet Blue or the stores of Abercrombie & Fitch. What they have in common is a focus on experience.

Experience marketing is a new and exciting concept. And it is not only of interest to academics. Marketing practitioners have come to realize that understanding how consumers experience brands and, in turn, how to provide appealing brand experiences for them, is critical for differentiating their offerings in a competitive marketplace.

1

Understanding consumer experiences is therefore a core task for consumer research. But, consumer and marketing research on experience is still emerging. Experience, as a concept and as an empirical phenomenon, is not as established as other consumer and marketing concepts such as choice, attitudes, consumer satisfaction, or brand equity.

This needs to change. In his Presidential address at the 2009 Association for Consumer Research Conference, Chris Janiszewski presented a passionate plea for an increased study of consumer experiences (Janiszewski, 2009). "So what is our opportunity? In what substantive areas do we, as a discipline, have a special interest and a competitive advantage?" he asked. "The answer is 'consumer experience.' . . . Where do we have a differential advantage with respect to our interest, our expertise, and our areas of application? I contend that it is not in the 'utility of choice' (expected utility), but the 'utility of consumption' (experienced utility or *subjective value)*." Most importantly, he argued that, "Benefits are not in the products. Benefits are in the consumer experience."

The study of experience is benefitted by the fact that multiple disciplines conduct research on the effect of experience. For example, consumer behavior has three core specialization areas: information processing, behavioral decision theory, and consumer culture theory; as we will see, they have all provided consumer insight on experiences. Researchers in the two other main disciplines of marketing — marketing models and marketing strategy — have also contributed to consumer experience research and to experience marketing. Moreover, the study of consumer behavior and marketing, and thus work on experience, is open to contributions from adjoining disciplines — for example, psychology, linguistics, economics, management, and sociology (MacInnis and Folkes, 2010). Finally, many experience concepts and ideas have come from management and practical writings. In this monograph, I will therefore cast a wide web, reviewing and discussing experience research conducted in various disciplines and in sub-disciplines of marketing.

I will begin with an exploration of the experience concept itself. What do we mean by "experience"? What are consumer experiences, and how are they different from other, established constructs in our field? Next, I will review some key concepts of experience marketing and empirical research findings that provide consumer insights on experiences. I will then turn to the strategic management and marketing literature on customer experience and the practical frameworks for managing experiences. Finally, I will explore an exciting emerging area of research — the interface of consumer experience and happiness.

# 2

## The Experience Concept

**ex.pe.ri.ence**

L *experientia*, fr. *experient-*, *experiens* (pres. part. of *experiri* to try)

1 *obs* **a**: a trial or test **b**: a tentative trial **c**: a conclusive proof;

2 : direct observation of or participation in events: an encountering, undergoing, or living through things in general as they take place in the course of time;

3 **a**: the state, extent, duration, or result of being engaged in a particular activity (as a profession) or in affairs, **b** *obs*: something approved by or made on the basis of such experience;

4 : knowledge, skill, or practice derived from direct observation of or participation in events: practical wisdom resulting from what one has encountered, undergone, or lived;

5 **a**: the sum total of the conscious events that make up an individual life, **b**: the sum total of events that make up the past of a community or nation or that have occurred within the knowledge of mankind generally;

6 : something personally encountered, undergone, or lived through, as **a**: an event observed or participated in, **b(1)**: a state of mind that forms a significant and often crucial part of

one's inner religious life and that is sometimes accompanied by intense emotion, (**2**): an account of such an experience, **c**: illicit sexual relations;

**7** : something by which one is stimulated or moved;

**8** *philos* **a**: the act or process of perceiving or apprehending, **b**: the content or the particular result of such experience, **c**: the discriminative reaction or the nonconscious response of an organism to events or happenings within its environment

*Webster's Third New International Dictionary* (Gove, 1976, p. 800)

The term "experience" has been used in various ways. The various definitions may be placed into two categories: some of them refer to the past (referring to knowledge and accumulated experiences over time) and others refer to ongoing perceptions and feelings and direct observation. In the English language, as in many Romanic languages (French, Spanish, and Italian), there is only one term to refer to both. Other languages use two separate lexicalized items — for example, *erfahrung* and *erlebnis* (in German); or keiken and taiken (in Japanese).

The experience term, with its multiple meanings, is also used in the business vocabulary. Some of its usages in marketing refer to experience in the sense of accumulated knowledge (e.g., "experience curve"); other usages seem to refer to direct observation or the necessity thereof (e.g., "experience goods"). In this monograph, which is focused on experience marketing, I will use the term to refer to experiences in the here and now — perceptions, feelings, and thoughts that consumers have when they encounter products and brands in the marketplace and engage in consumption activities — as well as the memory of such experiences.

What is the exact nature of these experiences? What are the key characteristics of experiences in general and, specifically, of consumer experiences?

## 2.1   Experience in Philosophy and Psychology

The field of philosophy has made important contributions toward understanding the nature of experience. For example, Danish philosopher Søren Kierkegaard tied experience to emotions (albeit, mostly negative and existential ones such as anxiety and despair). In current marketing research, affect and emotions are considered important experiences that guide consumer decision making.

Moreover, Kierkegaard stressed that experiences are subjective. For him, subjectivity is the unique relation that a person has with the outside, objective world. Subjectivity also includes the consciousness of a self which has a past, a present, and a future. For Kierkegaard not only objective matters have truth. A subjective experience also has truth for an individual. Alluding to a popular aphorism, one might say, "Experience is reality." Marketers must closely consider and understand this subjective reality, and the truth that it holds for an individual.

Philosophers and psychologists in the phenomenological tradition, for example, Husserl (1931) and Brentano (1874/1973), argue that experiences are "of" or "about" something; they have reference and intentionality. They are private events that occur in response to some stimulation. They are often not self-generated (as some thoughts and cognitions) but induced. Following such phenomenological insights, marketing scholars have focused not only on internal consumer processes — that is, the consumer psychology of experiences — but they have also paid attention to the stimuli that evoke consumer experiences.

Finally, American philosopher John Dewey (Dewey, 1925), belonging to the philosophical tradition of pragmatism, argued that knowledge (classifying, analyzing, and reasoning) is only one part of an individual's experience with the world. In addition to intellectual determinations, resulting from knowledge, individuals also have sensory perceptions, feelings, and actions resulting from experiences. As we will see, Dewey's ideas led marketers to propose that there are different types of experiences that can be empirically distinguished and measured.

## 2.2 Consumption Experience

One of the first academic articles that discussed and conceptualized experiences in detail in marketing was Holbrook and Hirschman's (1982) "The Experiential Aspects of Consumption: Consumer Fantasies, Feelings, and Fun." Positioning their article against the hegemony of the information processing perspective in consumer research, Holbrook and Hirschman felt that information processing neglected important consumption phenomena that involve fantasies, feelings, and fun — including playful leisure activities, sensory pleasures, daydreams, aesthetic enjoyment, and emotional responses.

Following the philosophical insights described earlier, the authors argued that this experiential view is phenomenological in spirit and regards consumption as a subjective state of consciousness. In contrast to the information processing perspective which stresses product attributes, utilitarian functions, and conscious and verbal thought processes, Holbrook and Hirschman's (1982) experiential view emphasizes the symbolic meaning, subconscious processes, and nonverbal cues resulting from consumption.

In their experiential view, affect plays a key role, and not just as an influence on attitude and arousal but in terms of the full range of possible consumer emotions (e.g., love, hate, fear, joy, boredom, anxiety, pride, anger, lust, and guilt). Holbrook and Hirschman (1982) pointed out that they did not want to replace one theory with another; their approach was complementary ("neither problem-directed nor experiential components can safely be ignored"): "By focusing single-mindedly on the consumer as information processor, recent consumer research has tended to neglect the equally important experiential aspects of consumption, thereby limiting our understanding of consumer behavior. Future research should work toward redressing this imbalance by broadening our area of study to include some consideration of consumer fantasies, feelings, and fun." (p. 139).

## 2.3   Experience in Marketing Management

The practically oriented management literature in the late 1990s and 2000s largely followed Holbrook and Hirshman's view. In a book titled "Experiential Marketing," Schmitt (1999) contrasted traditional marketing's product-oriented focus on functional features and benefits with experience marketing's customer-oriented focus on experiences. Rather than focusing on narrowly defined product categories (e.g., shampoo, shaving cream, blow dryer, and perfume) and their features, Schmitt argued that experience marketers focus on consumption situations such as "grooming in the bathroom," and ask how products and brands can enhance the consumption experience. He argued that customers do not only engage in rational choice, but are just as frequently driven by emotions. As a consequence, Schmitt called for an eclectic, multi-method research approach to studying experiences that focuses on customer insight.

As a result, experience marketing is usually broadly defined as any form of customer-focused marketing activity that creates a connection to customers. Based on this broad view, experiences may be evoked by products, packaging, communications, in-store interactions, sales relationships, events, and the like. They may occur as a result of online or offline activities. Some writers, however, view experience marketing or customer experiences more narrowly, and apply the experience concept only to interactions, relationships, or event contexts. For example, Lasalle and Britton (2002, p. 30) define it as "an interaction, or series of interactions, between a customer and a product, a company or its representative that lead to a reaction." Kishka (2003) views experience management as a systematic approach to measuring and managing customer feedback. Pine and Gilmore (1999) refer to experiences as events that engage individuals in a personal way.

Based on a review of the "state-of-the-art literature on experience marketing," Gentile et al. (2007, p. 397) present the following definition:

> "The Customer Experience originates from a *set of interactions* between a customer and a product, a company, or part of its organization, which provoke a reaction. This experience is strictly *personal* and implies the customer's *involvement* at different levels (rational, emotional, sensorial, physical and spiritual. Its evaluation depends on the comparison between a customer's *expectations* and the *stimuli* coming from the interaction with the company and its offering in correspondence of the different *moments of contact or touch-points.*" [Note: emphases are by the authors; references in this quote are omitted.]

## 2.4   Differences from Other Constructs

The experience concept is, in part, related to, but also conceptually distinct from, other internal consumer constructs in marketing. As Brakus et al. (2009) discussed, in an article focused on brand experience, the experience construct differs from evaluative, affective, and associative constructs such as attitudes, involvement, attachment, and brand associations.

Attitudes are general evaluations based on beliefs or automatic affective reactions (Fishbein and Ajzen, 1975; Murphy and Zajonc, 1993). Experiences, in contrast, are not merely general evaluative judgments about the product or brand (e.g., "I like this product," "I like this brand"); they include specific sensations, feelings, cognitions and behavioral responses triggered by specific stimuli in the consumer's environment. These specific experiences may result, at times, in general evaluations and attitudes, especially evaluations of the experience itself (e.g., "I like the experience"). However, the overall attitude toward the experience captures only a very small part of the entire experience.

Experience also differs from motivational and affective concepts such as involvement, brand attachment or customer delight. Involvement is based on needs, values, and interests that motivate a consumer toward an object, for example, a brand. Antecedents of involvement include the perceived importance and personal relevance of a brand (Zaichkowsky, 1985). Experience does not presume a motivational state. Experiences can happen when consumers do not show interest in, or have a personal connection with, the brand. Moreover, brands that consumers are highly involved with are not necessarily brands that evoke the strongest experiences. Experience also differs from the effect of strong emotional bonds between a consumer and a brand (Thomson et al., 2005; Park and MacInnis, 2006; Park et al., 2010). In contrast to brand attachment, which often evokes strong emotions, experience is not merely an emotional relationship concept. Most experiences also include ordinary sensations, feelings, cognitions, and behavioral responses evoked by brand-related stimuli. Over time, brand experiences may result in emotional bonds, but emotions are only one internal outcome of the stimulation that evokes experiences. In contrast to customer delight (Oliver et al., 1997), experiences do not have to disconfirm expectations and be surprising; they may be expected or unexpected.

Finally, experiences, especially those tied to brands, are distinct from brand associations and brand image (Keller, 1993). Consumers associate brands with benefits, products, people, places, and many other objects as part of an associative network (Keller, 2003). For example, consider the process of associating a brand with traits and human characteristics (such as "warm or "competent"), or evaluating it along brand personality dimensions of sincerity, excitement, competence, sophistication or ruggedness (Aaker, 1997; Aaker et al., 2010). When consumers engage in such associative processes, they infer something about the brand (Johar et al., 2005). They do not *feel* sincere or excited about the brand; they merely project these traits onto the brand. A brand may thus be viewed as contributing to consumer knowledge and meaning, but may or may not create an actual consumer experience (Berry, 1999). Brand experiences are not just associations. Brand experiences are dynamic sensations, feelings, cognitions, and behavioral responses. Like brand associations, they may be stored in consumer memory after the experience in the "here and now." Most likely, experiences would be stored not only semantically, but episodically, thus preserving a trace, for example, of the sensations and emotions that made up the experience with the brand (Barsalou, 1999).

# 3

# Key Concepts of Experience Marketing

## 3.1 Experiential Value

One of the most fundamental concepts of experience marketing is that value does not only reside in the object of consumption (products and services), and in seeking out and processing information about such objects; value also lies in the experience of consumption. For example, there is a tradition of work on customer value in which value is viewed as an interactive and relativistic (personal, comparative, and situational) preference experience (Holbrook, 1999; Lemke et al., 2010).

Accordingly, researchers have distinguished between utilitarian (or functional) and hedonic (or experiential) value (Gentile et al., 2007). Babin et al. (1994) have developed a scale to measure the two values as outcomes of shopping activities. Shopping's utilitarian value results from task completion; its hedonic value results from enjoyment and entertainment. Shoppers who focus on the activity's utilitarian value consider it to be "work"; those focusing on its hedonic value consider it to be "fun." Relatedly, Voss et al. (2003) have constructed a scale that measures the utilitarian and hedonic dimensions of attitudes toward product categories and brands. The scale includes ten, seven-point semantic differential items; five refer to utilitarian attitudes and the other five refer to hedonic attitudes. The utilitarian items are effective/ineffective, helpful/unhelpful, functional/not functional, necessary/unnecessary, and practical/impractical. The hedonic items are fun/not fun, exciting/dull, delightful/not delightful, thrilling/not thrilling/ and enjoyable/unenjoyable.

One technique to identify utilitarian and experiential values is the "laddering technique." Laddering is a structured interview technique, with corresponding software to present the interview content, where consumers are asked what is important to them about a product or service. Then, through a series of "why" probes, the goal is to uncover consumer benefits and values that are linked to product attributes (Vriens and Hofstede, 2000). For example, the feature of whitening toothpaste may be tied to the aesthetic benefit of having better-looking teeth and ultimately to the relational value of achieving greater self-esteem or social acceptance. Over the course of a person's life, values may change. For example, as a student or early adult, a consumer may value utilitarian aspects of a hotel (a clean room and basic hotel facilities); later on in life, he or she may desire a certain aesthetic style and seek hotels for unique experiences tied to higher-order values (a stunning location in the middle of a rain forest with a spa and seemingly endless pool).

Pine and Gilmore (1998) have argued that economic value at a societal level has progressed through three stages, and that we are entering a fourth stage: the experience economy. The earliest stage, the commodity economy, was concerned with the extraction of various substances from the world around us. Next, starting with the Industrial Revolution in the 19th century, came the manufacturing economy, where the primary economic offering was the making of products. The manufacturing economy did not replace the commodity economy entirely, but added an additional kind of economic offering. In the twentieth century followed the service economy, where the offerings of highest value were the delivery of intangible services. Now, in the twenty-first century, many developed societies are entering the experience economy, where the highest-value economic offerings are experiences. In the experience economy, businesses stage memorable experiences for customers, which are entertaining and/or educational in nature.

Unfortunately, Pine and Gilmore (1999) provide no numbers on the size of the experience economy or empirical substantiation for the claim that economies are now entering a new stage of economic offerings. Raghunathan (2008) has questioned whether experiential offerings are qualitatively different from those in a service or a goods economy. By Pine and Gilmore's (1999) definition of experiences as "events," or economic offers that are event-like (such as "theme restaurants"), the experience economy constitutes only a small percentage of most economies. Rather than entering a new economic stage, it may be more appropriate to view business attention to experiences as a new way of marketing products and services, and even consumer commodities (such as salt, pepper, or produce). The experiential value would then not exist in the commodities, products or services *per se*, but in the marketing of these items.

## 3.2    Types of Consumer Experiences

Following Dewey's (1925) philosophical analyses, Schmitt (1999) presented five types of experience marketing approaches, referred to as "strategic experiential modules": "sense," "feel," "think," "act," and "relate."

According to Schmitt, "sense marketing" appeals to consumers' senses (sight, sound, touch, taste, and smell). "Feel marketing" appeals to customers' inner feelings and emotions, ranging from mildly positive moods linked to a brand (e.g., for a noninvolving, nondurable grocery brand or service or industrial product) to strong emotions of joy and pride (e.g., for a consumer durable, technology, or social marketing campaign). "Think marketing" appeals to the intellect in order to deliver cognitive, problem-solving experiences that engage customers creatively. "Act marketing" targets physical behaviors, lifestyles, and interactions. Finally, "relate marketing" creates experiences by taking into account individuals' desires to be part of a social context (e.g., to their self-esteem, being part of a subculture, or a brand community).

Dubé and LeBel (2003) have distinguished four similar "pleasure dimensions" — emotional, intellectual, physical, and social pleasures. Dubé and LeBel's (2003) four pleasure dimensions map closely to four of Schmitt's experience modules (namely, feel, think, act and relate, respectively).

Gentile et al. (2007) distinguished the following six experiential components:

- Sensorial (sight, hearing, touch, taste, and smell experiences and how they arouse aesthetic pleasure, excitement, satisfaction and a sense of beauty)
- Emotional (moods, feelings, and emotional experiences that create an affective relation with the company, its brands and products)
- Cognitive (experiences related to thinking and conscious mental processes to get customers to use their creativity or problem solving so that they revise assumptions about a product)
- Pragmatic (experiences resulting from the practical act of doing something and usability)
- Lifestyle (experiences resulting from the affirmation of values and personal beliefs)
- Relational (experiences, emerging from social contexts and relationships, that occur during common consumption as part of a real or imagined community or to affirm social identity)

As can be seen, Gentile et al. (2007) added a new dimension, the pragmatic component, based on the design-oriented literature on user experience and human-object interactions. However, they did not empirically test the model (in terms of its dimensionality and in terms of the discriminant validity of the pragmatic component, for example). In fact, in their empirical research with actual brands (e.g., iPod), not all components could be verified as independent through a factor analysis but showed overlaps (e.g., between sensorial components and lifestyle, or among pragmatic, cognitive, and lifestyle components).

Gentile et al. (2007) did provide, however, the results of a survey that showed that the sensorial component was the most important one across several experiential brands (Swatch, Pringles, Harley-Davidson, Smart, iPod, Nike, HC Brands Bar, Playstation, Gatorade, McDonald's

Ikea, Swarowski). Yet, "complex experiences," which involve more than a single component, emerged for many brands. An interpretive analysis revealed that each product leveraged more than one component, and the particular combination depended on the characteristics of the product itself. The components are, according to the authors, not activated independently, but have overlapping areas and interrelations. The study may be considered rather exploratory, but it raises intriguing possibilities regarding the highly interactive nature of complex — or "holistic" — experiences.

Brakus et al. (2009) based their work on brand experiences, in part, on the five modules distinguished by Schmitt (1999). They viewed these modules, however, not only as strategic devices, but as internal and behavioral outcomes, and defined brand experiences as "subjective, internal consumer responses (sensations, feelings, and cognitions) as well as behavioral responses evoked by brand-related stimuli that are part of a brand's design and identity, packaging, communications and environments" (Brakus et al., 2009, p. 53). They constructed a scale to measure experiences and explored its dimensionality. Four experiential dimensions could be validated in qualitative and quantitative research: sensory, affective, intellectual, and behavioral experiences.

Table 3.1 shows the items of the so-called Brand Experience Scale. The scale is relatively short, consisting of only 12 items. Psychometrically, the scale is internally consistent and consistent across samples and studies. The scale also passed several reliability tests such as test–retest reliability, criterion validity, and discriminant validity from other scales (including brand evaluations, brand involvement, brand attachment, customer delight, and brand personality).

Zarantonello and Schmitt (2010) used the Brand Experience Scale to identify individual differences among consumers and to profile them. Using cluster analysis, five clusters emerged: "hedonistic consumers," "action-oriented consumers," "holistic consumers," "inner-directed consumers," and "utilitarian consumers."

In sum, in the experience literature, there is a consensus that it is useful to conceptualize experiences along multiple experience dimensions. These experience dimensions include sensory-affective, cognitive-intellectual, and behavior and action-oriented components. Moreover,

Table 3.1.    Brand experience scale.

| | |
|---|---|
| *SENSORY* | This brand makes a strong impression on my visual sense or other senses. |
| | I find this brand interesting in a sensory way. |
| | This brand does not appeal to my sense. |
| *AFFECTIVE* | This brand induces feelings and sentiments. |
| | I do not have strong emotions for this brand. |
| | This brand is an emotional brand. |
| *BEHAVIORAL* | I engage in physical actions and behaviors when I use this brand. |
| | This brand results in bodily experiences. |
| | This brand is not action oriented. |
| *INTELLECTUAL* | I engage in a lot of thinking when I encounter this brand. |
| | This brand does not make me think. |
| | This brand stimulates my curiosity and problem solving. |

*Source*: Brakus, J. J., B. H. Schmitt and L. Zarantonello (2009), Brand experience: What is it? How is it measured? Does it affect loyalty? *Journal of Marketing* **73** (may), 52–68.

because experiences are evoked by environmental cues, social and relational elements are also important aspects of experiences. From a research perspective, it is critical to examine the impact of experiences not only in the aggregate, but additionally, dimensions of experiences must be examined in terms of how they relate to certain outcome variables. And from a practical perspective, it is key to identify the most appropriate positioning of a brand along various experience dimensions.

## 3.3    Ordinary and Extraordinary Experiences

Another key distinction in experience marketing concerns the unusualness of the experience. Ordinary experiences occur as part of everyday life; they are routine and result, to a degree, from passive stimulation. Extraordinary experiences are more active, intense, and stylized. Extraordinary experiences have been referred to as "flow" (Csikszentmihalyi, 1990), "peak experiences" (Privette, 1983), "epiphanies" (Denzin, 1992) and "transcendent customer experiences" (Schouten et al., 2007).

Flow, peak experiences, epiphanies, and transcendent experiences differ to some degree. Both flow and peak experiences are achieved through intense and focused activity, and absorption or immersion in those activities, thereby raising an experience to extraordinary levels. While Csikszentmihalyi largely describes flow as an internal process, peak experiences are more likely to originate from the outside. Overwhelmed by nature, or an unexpected emotional gesture, individuals feel connected with a "larger-than-life" phenomenon. In moments of epiphanies, an experience leads individuals to redefine themselves. Transcendent customer experiences provoke radical re-definitions of the self, resulting from major upheavals, crisis situations, or an intense memory and relived moment.

The distinction between extraordinary versus ordinary experiences is reminiscent of the distinction between the "sacred" and the "profane" in consumer culture theory (Belk et al., 1989). The sacred in consumption is the opposite of the ordinary routine of everyday life. The sacred is beyond analytics and rationalization and can only be understood through devotion. Similar to the sacred, extraordinary experiences can be devotional and momentarily ecstatic.

Detailed analyses of extraordinary experiences have been conducted through interpretive research — among river rafters (Arnould and Price, 1993), sky divers (Loeffler, 2004), and Harley Davidson motorcyclists (Schouten and McAlexander, 1995). Extraordinary experiences may also be aesthetic experiences which may occur during a classical music concert, in art or by viewing landscapes. Extraordinary experiences include extreme emotions, are often communal in nature, and transformational for consumers.

For example, Schouten et al. (2007) have characterized "transcendent customer experiences" (TCE) as including feelings such as self-transformation, separation from the ordinary and mundane, and connectedness to larger phenomena outside one's self. "TCEs are marked by emotional intensity, epiphany, singularity, and newness of experience, extreme enjoyment, oneness, ineffability, extreme focus of attention, and the testing of personal limits" (p. 358). They have developed a TCE scale and shown that TCEs are critical for the integration of a brand community and for building brand loyalty among brand community members. Arnould and Price (1993) studied the extraordinary experience of multi-day river rafting trips in the Colorado River basin, a growing component of the Colorado leisure services industry. Using multiple methods, they showed that extraordinary experiences such as river rafting provide personal growth and self-renewal, create a sense of "communitas" (a "sacred" sense of community and camaraderie), and a strong feeling of harmony with nature. In Loeffler's (2004) study of high-risk leisure consumption (such as skydiving, climbing, and BASE jumping), he found similar motivations and themes and laid out the evolution of various motives (from thrill to achievement to personal identity, flow and communitas). In this set of extraordinary experiences, even death is seen as part of life. As one of the skydivers interviewed put it, "We do not have a death wish, we have a life wish! A wish to live life to the fullest, and if by chance we do die skydiving, then at least we died doing what we loved" (Loeffler, 2004, p. 19).

Caru and Cova (2003) have argued that the obsession with extraordinary experiences constitutes an American ideology and has become a "cult of strong emotions" (p. 279). They suggest that researchers focus as well on simpler and more contemplative consumption experiences such as walking and having time with oneself, instead of expecting consumers to fill each moment of life with ordinary or extraordinary product and service experiences. Rather than planning experiences for consumers, this alternative view calls for letting consumers construct their own experiences.

## 3.4 Experience Touchpoints

Experiences occur at various information collection, decision, and consumption stages. Lasalle and Britton (2002) have presented an experience engagement model consisting of five stages. The experience engagement model is similar to earlier consumer decision models in marketing (Howard and Sheth, 1969). The five stages are:

- Discover (i.e., the consumer identifies products and services to meet specific wants and needs)
- Evaluate (i.e., the consumer examines the possible choices identified, compares them and, using various decision and choice rules, narrows them down to a preferred choice)

- Acquire (i.e., the consumer expands money and time to shop for and buy the product)
- Integrate (i.e., the consumer integrates the purchase into his or her daily life, e.g., by using services around the product)
- Extend (i.e., the continuing relationship and bonds a consumer makes with a brand)

At each of these stages, there are touchpoints between the company, and its products and services, and consumers, which may result in experiences. Davis and Longoria (2003) present a "brand touchpoint wheel" including prepurchase, purchase, and postpurchase experience phases, and have identified such touchpoints within each phase.

- Pre-purchase touchpoints include advertising, public relations, web sites, new media, direct mail/samples, coupons and incentives, deals and promotions.
- Purchase touchpoints include packaging, point-of-purchase displays, store and shelf placements, salespeople and sales environments.
- Post-purchase touchpoints include product and package performance, customer service, newsletters, and loyalty programs.

Frow and Payne (2007) list methodologies for identifying and mapping touchpoints, including process mapping (Shostack, 1987), service-blueprinting (Kingman-Brundage, 1989) and customer-firm touchpoint analysis (Sawhney et al., 2004).

Research may be conducted at each experience touchpoint in terms of the experience that it creates. For example, take the sales environment. Here, research has been conducted on "atmospherics" (Babin and Attaway, 2000; Bitner, 1992; Turley and Milliman, 2000) and in-store experiences (Backstrom and Johansson, 2006; Mathwick et al., 2002; Spies et al., 1997). In a retail context, the customer experience includes, for example, the store atmosphere, the service interface, assortment and merchandising. Verhoef et al. (2009) identify a wide range of future research issues related to experiential aspects in sales environments.

Regarding packaging and product designs, Orth and Malkewitz (2008) have studied packaging for wines and fragrances, and provided examples for many other categories (cereal, detergents, soft drinks, soups, and tea). They identified five design types: Massive, contrasting, natural, delicate, and nondescript designs. These types are related to brand personalities. They find that "sincere brands should have natural packaging design, exciting brands should have contrasting designs, competent brands should have delicate designs, sophisticated brands should have natural or delicate designs, and rugged brands should have contrasting or massive designs" (Orth and Malkewitz, 2008, p. 64).

Experience touchpoints may be further broken down into constituent stimuli that evoke experiences (names, logos, designs, store elements, etc.). They are often referred to as *experiential stimuli*.

Apple Computers has prominently used experiential attributes as part of its product design and environments and in its communications for many years. In the early days, its logo featured the colors of a rainbow. Nowadays the logo is usually monochrome but much brighter. Early on, for the Macintosh computer, Apple used a smiley face that appeared on the screen of computers when they were powered up. More recently, the company used translucent colors to differentiate, for example, its iMac and iPod lines from competitive products. Screensavers, too, have become increasingly colorful and aesthetically appealing. In addition, Apple has integrated the logos, colors, and shapes of its product design with the design of its web sites and its so-called AppleStores. Similar approaches focusing on colors, shapes or other experiential stimuli have been used by many other global and local brands in all sorts of product categories.

Each experiential stimulus can be quite complex with respect to its structure and experiential impact. Take a simple element like typeface, which appears at many touchpoints. Henderson et al. (2004) have shown that typeface design has six underlying design dimensions: elaborate, harmony, natural, flourish, weight, and compressed. Also, studying 195 logos, Henderson and Cote (1998) found that multiple dimensions determine the impact of logos: high-recognition logos should be very natural, very harmonious, and moderately elaborate whereas high-image logos should be moderately elaborate and natural.

Henderson et al. (2003) have largely replicated these results in an international context. In addition, there are colors (Bellizzi et al., 1983; Bellizzi and Hite, 1992; Degeratu et al., 2000; Gorn et al., 1997; Meyers-Levy and Peracchio, 1995) and shapes (Veryzer, Jr. and Hutchinson, 1998) that influence experience. Together with typefaces and logos, they appear, for example, at various experience touchpoints such as in graphic designs of slogans and messages, as graphic elements on web sites and in backgrounds of shopping environments. Thus, to identify all the stimuli that can evoke experiences at various touchpoints is a complex research task, and selecting the right touchpoint stimuli is a challenging management task.

# 4

---

## Consumer Research Issues

---

The experience concept raises several consumer research issues. For example, many experiences unfold over time. Do consumers prefer experiences to be split up or to be continuous? How are experiences remembered? Moreover, can consumers have positive and negative experiences at the same time? How do they process experiential attributes? Finally, can experiences be rational?

### 4.1 Do Individuals Prefer Experiences to be Interrupted or to be Continuous?

Nelson and Meyvis (2008) ask you to imagine undergoing a painful physical therapy session or enjoying a relaxing massage. They then ask you to imagine, whether you would prefer to break up the therapy session and, if you did, whether the break would make the session more painful or less painful. They also ask you to imagine the same for the pleasant experience of the massage.

If you are like the participants in their six studies, you will indicate a preference, before you have the experience, to break it up if it is a negative experience but to keep a positive experience intact. But you are fooling yourself because, Nelson and Meyvis (2008) also found that inserting a break into a negative experience makes it worse, and taking a break in a positive experience makes it better.

Why is that so? Nelson and Meyvis (2008) propose that breaks disrupt adaptation and intensify the experience following the break. That's great for positive experiences but not good for negative experiences. Why, however, Nelson and Meyvis (2008) ask, do people never adapt to life near a highway? Perhaps because people who live close to a highway experience the permanent change from loud to quiet as a never-ending sequence of breaks.

## 4.2    How do Consumers Remember Experiences?

Investigating so-called experience profiles, many studies have found that when individuals summarize and evaluate experiences in memory, they do not simply average or combine the experiences in the entire sequence — for example, by following a discounted utility model. Rather, individuals extract certain defining features — or gestalt characteristics — of these sequences.

Specifically, overall evaluations seem to be most strongly influenced by momentary experiences at the most intense (i.e., peak) moments and final moments (Ariely and Carmon, 2000; Fredrickson and Kahneman, 1993; Varey and Kahneman, 1992). Moreover, individuals also greatly care about improvements or deteriorations over time.

Unexpected memory-driven effects have been reported for variety seeking of experiences as well. Traditional variety-seeking models assume that individuals choose, each day, the experience that provides the most pleasure. Ratner et al. (1999) showed, however, that consumers switch away from a favorite experience even if they get less pleasure from the switch than they would from a stay. The reason for this effect seems to be that individuals favor building memories of a variety of sequences. Take the example of a vacation. A person may anticipate that the pleasure from the overall vacation, when looking back, may be greater if there is some variety.

## 4.3 Can Positive and Negative Experiences Exist Simultaneously?

We know that people try to pursue pleasure and avoid pain. But how can this hedonistic assumption be reconciled with the obvious enjoyment (by some) of certain experiences that elicit negative feelings of fear, disgust, and terror — such as watching horror movies? Can individuals experience negative and positive affect at the same time?

In several experiments, Andrade and Cohen (2007) have shown that individuals can co-activate negative and positive affect. This happens when individuals are in a so-called "protective frame" — they detach themselves from the danger that seems to be present, and are confident they can handle it or understand that the situation poses no real danger. Although the authors empirically limited themselves to horror movies, they argue that their findings are relevant as well for all experiences that encompass fearfulness (e.g., extreme sports and other extraordinary experiences discussed earlier).

At a milder level of intensity, feeling both good and bad at the same time also seems to be quite common in indulgences. When we buy a luxury good, indulge in a creamy, high-calorie dessert, or waste time doing nothing, we may feel good but also experience feelings of stress, guilt, and regret. In a food consumption context, Ramanathan and Williams (2007) gave undergraduate students an indulgent cookie and showed that their experienced emotions–both "hedonic" (i.e., spontaneous) and "self-conscious" (i.e., higher-order) — were quite complex. While both impulsive and prudent people experience ambivalent hedonic emotions (both positive, e.g., pleasure and delight, and negative, e.g., stress, emotions at the same time), they were ambivalent for different reasons: impulsive people are ambivalent purely because of the presence of these conflicting hedonic emotions, but prudent people are ambivalent because of both the hedonic emotions and negative self-conscious emotions (e.g., regret and guilt). Also, while both impulsive and prudent people experience less ambivalence after a delay, impulsive people experience a sharp decline of the negative emotions (both hedonic and self-conscious) but prudent people experience a drop of the positive emotions. This in turn affects the propensity to indulge again: impulsive people seem to be resigned to such ambivalence happening again (after having indulged in a cookie, they still choose potato chips) but prudent people want to launder their negative emotions (after a cookie they choose a notebook rather than potato chips).

## 4.4    How are Experiential Attributes Processed?

In an award winning article in the *Journal of Marketing Research* entitled "Meaningful Brands from Meaningless Differentiation: The Dependence on Irrelevant Attributes," Carpenter et al. (1994) wrote:

> "[Michael] Porter describes differentiation as developing a unique position on an attribute that is 'widely valued by buyers.' However, many brands also successfully differentiate on an attribute that *appears* [Note: emphasis by the original authors] valuable but, on closer examination, is irrelevant to creating the implied benefit. For example, Procter & Gamble differentiates instant Folger's coffee by its 'flaked coffee crystals' created through a 'unique, patented process,' implying (but not stating) in its advertising that flaked coffee crystals improve the taste of coffee. In fact, the shape of the coffee particle is relevant for ground coffee (greater surface area exposed during brewing extracts more flavor), but it is irrelevant for instant coffee: The crystal simply dissolves, so its surface area does not affect flavor. Similarly, Alberto Culver differentiates its Alberto Natural Silk Shampoo by including silk in the shampoo, and advertising it with the slogan, 'We put silk in a bottle' to suggest a user's hair will be silky. However a company spokesman conceded that silk 'doesn't really do anything for hair.' Consumers apparently value these differentiating attributes even though they are, in one sense, irrelevant." [Note: the references in the quote have been excluded.] (p. 339).

The authors were surprised when they found that what they called "meaningless differentiation" was valued by consumers in a surprising number of situations. In some cases, increasing price even increased preference for the meaninglessly differentiated brand. Most surprisingly, the competitive advantage created by adding an irrelevant attribute could be sustained even when consumers acknowledged that the differentiating attribute is irrelevant.

These findings are surprising only if viewed from a functional and utilitarian point of view. From an experiential marketing perspective, there is nothing surprising here. Flaked coffee crystals, silk in a shampoo bottle — as well as some of the other brand attributes that were used in the experiment, such as authentic Milanese-style pasta, Alpine-class down-filled jackets, and studio-designed signal processing systems for compact disc players — are only meaningless from a functional perspective. From an experiential perspective, one can say that such descriptions use imagery and colorful language to communicate about the brand. These descriptions *imply* functionality. Thus, consumers confer value to them through an inferential process based on this implied functionality.

Yet, there are also some attributes that deliver or imply no functionality or functional utility whatsoever. We referred to them earlier as *experiential attributes.*

We know a lot about how consumers process functional attributes: deliberately, reason-based, step-by-step, goal-directed and as trade-offs (Broniarczyk and Alba, 1994; Brown and Carpenter, 2000; Shafir et al., 1993; Simonson, 1989; Chernev, 2001; Fischer et al., 1999). But how exactly do consumers process experiential attributes? How do these experiential attributes create value, relative to functional attributes?

Brakus et al. (2008) examined how experiential attributes are processed and how they have value in consumer decision making. Using computer diskettes, they showed four choice situations to consumers: (1) A control condition where the decision was between two functional disks; (2) one where the decision included a decision between a purely functional disk with superior function and a disk that was functionally inferior but had a sensory experiential attribute (a nice translucent green instead of the standard black); (3) one where the decision included a functionally superior disk and a functionally inferior but affectively experiential disk (with a smiley face on the diskette), and (4) a situation where the two diskettes were functionally identical, but one had the green color and the other the smiley. In addition, they also varied so-called contextual cues through a banner advertisement.

As expected, consumers engaged in deliberate, analytical, comparison-like processing for the functional attributes in the control condition. However, in the conditions where an experiential attribute was present, they sometimes engaged in deliberate processing, just as they did for functional attributes, but they also circumvented deliberation by responding in a direct and immediate way without consciously labeling the stimulus as a specific attribute.

The technical term for this kind of processing is "processing fluency" (Winkielman et al., 2003). Fluent processes are involved, for example, in spontaneous visual categorization and discrimination (Grunert, 1996; Schneider and Shiffrin, 1977; Tulving and Schacter, 1990). Fluent processes also occur when people engage in simple congruency matching tasks (Kelley and Jacoby, 1998; Roediger, 1990), for example when individuals discriminate one stimulus type from another (e.g., color from shape) or when they distinguish one stimulus category from another (e.g., visually presented experiential stimuli from textually presented functional information) (Edell and Staelin, 1983; Houston et al., 1987; Shepard, 1967). Fluent processing of stimuli also results in more positive judgments for a variety of stimuli (Winkielman et al., 2003).

In sum, whereas functional attributes are processed deliberately, consumers have a choice when they process experiential attributes: they can process experiential attributes deliberately or fluently. It turns out that there are two factors that determine whether experiential attributes are processed deliberately or fluently. The first factor relates to the set of alternatives, specifically the nature of the functional attributes that are part of the product description: whether they are diagnostic or not (Shafir et al., 1993; Simonson, 1989). The second factor relates to the judgment context (the environment in which the judgment takes place), specifically the type of contextual cues that can prime experiential attributes: whether they are of a matching or non-matching stimulus type.

## 4.5 Can Experiences be Rational?

From a rational and normative point of view, experience may be viewed with suspicion. Behavioral decision theory has provided ample evidence for peoples neglect, or insufficient consideration, of statistically presented "base-rate" information compared to vividly or saliently presented experiential information (Gilovich et al., 2002).

Thus, with good reason, Hoch (2002) views experiences as "seductive"; they are intense and highly memorable. And consumers put more value on experience than they should. He writes, "Personal experience is overrated. People find it more compelling than they should. In many consumption situations, people are too trusting of what they have learned through experience, seduced by the very real nature of an ongoing stream of activity." (Hoch, 2002, p. 448).

In a similar vein, German philosopher Imanuel Kant, many centuries ago, contrasted experience with reason. In Book 1, Section 1 of the "Critique of Pure Reason," (Kant, 1781/1848) Kant put it even more bluntly than Hoch: "For nothing more prejudicial and more unworthy of a philosopher, can be found, than the vulgar appeal to a pretended contrary experience." (Kant, 1781/1848, p. 250).

On the other hand, there may be logic and rationality to feelings, and perhaps other subjective experiences. Pham (2004) proposed that feelings may tap into a separate, but not necessarily less logical system of judgment. Thus, any generalized statement about the rationality or irrationality of feelings may be not called for (Pham, 2007). It is not easy to show and to specify under what conditions people might make superior decisions against an objective standard when they rely on their feelings rather than analytical thinking. However, it was shown that when choosing among certain objects — namely artistic objects, such as posters of paintings by Monet and Van Gogh — people were less satisfied with their personal choice when asked to think about their reason of choice. People seem to have focused on attributes that are easy to verbalize rather than on the core, perhaps experiential, reasons of their original choice (Wilson et al., 1993). Feelings can also provide information, and consumers can use the informational value of feelings as a heuristic: "I feel good about it: I must like it" Schwarz (1990). Feelings also allow for faster judgments, and their preferences can be more consistent (Lee et al., 2009; Pham et al., 2001).

More importantly, relying on your feelings may make you richer. When people rely on their feelings in the standard ultimatum game, they can make more money (Stephen and Pham, 2008). In this game, two players have to divide a sum of money. The first player proposes how to divide the sum between the two players. The second player can either accept or reject this proposal. If the second player rejects, neither player receives anything. If the second player accepts, the money is split according to the first player's proposal. Stephen and Pham (2008) found that players who demonstrated more trust in their feelings had higher average returns than players with lower trust in their feelings. This seems to be because the proposers who rely on their feelings focus more on the offers themselves rather than the potential outcomes of their offers. Moreover, people may be able to predict the stock market better. People who had higher trust in their feelings were able to predict the Dow Jones Industrial Average stock market index more accurately than those that had lower trust in their feelings (Pham et al., 2011).

Experiences just seem to be magical.

# 5

## Customer Experience Management

The experience concept has received attention not only in academic writings, it is also a concept that is analyzed and utilized in business practices. Customer Experience Management — a set of frameworks, tools, and methodologies to manage customer experiences — has been applied in many industries. Kambhammettu (2005) offers examples from the finance, mobile phone, and airline industries. Here I will describe some of the most common management frameworks presented in managerially-oriented journals or books and used in management and marketing practice.

## 5.1 Experience Engineering

In 1994 Steve Haeckel, then the chair of trustees of the Marketing Science Institute, and Lou Carbone, an Adjunct Faculty Member at the IBM Advanced Business Institute, collaborated on a seminal early article on experience management, published in *Marketing Management*, a quarterly business publication of the American Marketing Association. In the article titled "Engineering Customer Experiences," they defined experience as "the 'take-away' impression formed by people's encounters with products, services and businesses — a perception produced when humans consolidate sensory information" (Carbone and Haeckel, 1994, p. 1). They stressed that engineering experiences requires new management principles, tools, and methodologies. Moreover, they argued that the focus of this new approach must be the total experience as the key customer value proposition.

Carbone (2004) expanded experience engineering into "clued-in management." He argued that managing the signals — or "clues" — being emitted throughout a customer experience will be a source of competitive advantage. According to Carbone (2004), "experience management is a completely integrated set of disciplines that seeks to identify the clues — rational and emotional, humanistic and mechanic — that customers consciously and unconsciously wish to find in their encounters." (p. 97). Clued-in management begins when firms develop an understanding of the sensory clues that customers process and interpret, and the role that such clues play in creating experiential value.

Clue management includes managing the breadth and depth of the experience (how far it can be extended and how deep or detailed it is). It also includes managing what Carbone calls the "humanic clues" (e.g., interactions with people) and the "mechanical clues" (e.g., environmental design).

The focus of the clued-in approach is mostly targeted toward managing sensory clues that contribute to the cumulative sense of the experience. These individual clues can be combined into "clue clusters" and entire "clue systems." There may be interactions among clues. Clue interaction is multiplicative, not additive. Just one significant negative or nonexistent clue can jeopardize the value of the entire experience.

Various methods are used in clue management and discussed by Carbone (2004). "Clue scan" is a sensory review of the physical environment, processes and "humanic" behaviors of the various layers of the experience. "Experience mapping" is a service blueprint that describes, in detail, the actions that a customer goes through during a service encounter (e.g., gets off flight, stops in restroom, looks for bag claim, waits for baggage, gets baggage, looks for car rental, waits for van, and so on). Observational research records what people do when they have an experience. In-depth interviews can examine the value of the experience that customers are getting. ZMET, a tool developed by Zaltman and Coulter (1995), is used to uncover deep and often unconscious meanings.

## 5.2 The Experience Economy

As described earlier, in the *Experience Economy*, Pine and Gilmore (1999) defined experiences as event marketing. In line with the view that experience management is primarily event management, they suggested that managers should view themselves as theater producers who stage events for consumers using various types of theater formats. In an article in the *Harvard Business Review*, and a book, they provided a typology of theaters (and events), differentiated along two dimensions: the first encompasses performances that are either stable (the same each time) or dynamic (changing each time), and the second covers whether the audience itself is stable or dynamic (i.e., likely to provide feedback and input that must be incorporated into the performance). The resulting four types that managers may choose when staging and producing experiences are:

1. *Platform theater.* This form of theater, or event production, is the traditional format with a staged performance, where the script does not vary, and the performance is done in front of a noninteractive audience.
2. *Street theater.* Street theater has traditionally been the domain of jugglers, mimes, and clowns. Here, the script is stable but the audience is dynamic.
3. *Matching theater.* Matching theater, exemplified by film and television, requires the integration of work outcomes. The end product results from piecing together distinct portions of work that may be performed at different times and in different places.
4. *Improvisation theater.* The process of improvising requires that a performer have certain dynamic skills, in terms of thinking on one's feet and responding to new and changing demands from the audience.

## 5.3   The CEM Framework

In *Customer Experience Management*, Schmitt (2003) presented the CEM framework, a project-based framework for managing experiences. The original CEM framework was made up of five steps (an analysis step, a strategy step and three implementation steps). For the purpose of this monograph, we can simplify the framework into three basic steps:

1. Analyzing the experiential world of the customer.
2. Building the experience platform.
3. Implementing the experience.

### 5.3.1   Analyzing the Experiential World of the Customer

The research and analysis of step 1 — referred to as "customer insight" — is done from a broad perspective by analyzing and researching not only the brand, but also consumption and usage patterns of customers and the socio-cultural context that affects consumers' experiential needs and wants. Customer-insight research can include focus groups, surveys and interviews but is frequently supplemented by ethnographic and interpretive research techniques. In contrast to laddering techniques, the analysis of the experiential world does not begin with the brand, from which one then ladders up to personal values. Rather, the analysis begins with the socio-cultural context of the consumer, or in a B2B context with business trends, and then applies these insights to the brand. For example, the socio-cultural analysis may include trends such as "wellness," "spiritualism," or "naturalism" that influence consumer lifestyles, and, ultimately, perceptions of skin care and cosmetics products and brands. This technique is referred to as "funneling."

### 5.3.2   Building the Experience Platform

The second step, the experience platform, includes the formulation of a core experience concept that can be used as a guiding principle for subsequent implementations. The concept must resonate with consumers and be in line with the brand's values and personality (Aaker, 1996).

An experience platform is different from a positioning statement or perceptual map. The experiential platform includes a dynamic, multi-sensory, multi-dimensional depiction of the desired experience (referred to as "experiential positioning") and a specification of the experiential value that the customer can expect from the product (the "experiential value promise") — for example, in terms of the types of experiences (or experience dimensions) discussed earlier. The experiential platform culminates in a sensory implementation theme that can be used to coordinate marketing and communication efforts.

For example, the above mentioned concepts of wellness, spirituality, and naturalness may result in a positioning platform of "skin energy" that provides sensory and emotional value. In communicating such a position, a company may use visual and verbal concepts (images of water, forests, yoga and the like) as themes at various touchpoints.

### 5.3.3 Implementing the Experience

Finally, the experience platform must be implemented in a brand experience and in customer interfaces (in a store, online, in a call center, etc.). Designing the brand experience includes, among other things, the selection of experiential features. The experience also includes the selection of an overall "look and feel" in the brand's visual identity, packaging, web sites and in physical environments or stores. Verbal messages using an experiential language, as well as visuals in communications, complete the brand experience.

The design of the brand experience is often outsourced. It thus becomes the domain of corporate identity and design firms, graphic and interior designers, as well as media and advertising agencies. Various agencies communicate with one another to guarantee consistency and integration. Also, more and more firms are appointing "customer experience" or "brand experience" managers that make sure that integration across various experience touchpoints takes place.

After the experience project is finished, the experience should be managed on a continuous basis. It needs to be upgraded and updated. Ideally, the experience philosophy also needs to be institutionalized. This requires the alignment of organizational structures and processes, and, most importantly, of people and systems (Labovitz and Rosansky, 1997). Alignment is especially important in service businesses where employees directly interface with customers. Companies nowadays provide employees with incentives in order to motivate them to deliver the right experience. Finally, companies have begun to focus on the employee experience (Heska, 2009). This shows that experience management is no longer just a marketing issue; it is also a human resources management issue.

## 5.4   Additional Management Frameworks

In addition to these three frameworks, several other experience management frameworks have been proposed. Some of these frameworks are specifically focused on the management of certain kinds of experiences. For example, Schmitt and Simonson (1997), focusing on "marketing aesthetics," presented the "Corporate Expressions/Customer Impressions" (CE/CI) framework, which is a Brunswikian lens model for managing sensory experiences. The CE/CI framework proposed that customers do not have direct access to an organization's or brand's mission, values or personality. Customers only see the public face of the organization or brand — its expressions. Expressions include aesthetic styles (e.g., a minimalist design or natural look and feel) and themes (commercial symbols, narratives, and slogans). These expressions, in turn, lead to customer impressions and inferences about the organization's and the brand's mission, values or personality. Similarly, Lindstrom's (2005) "Brand Sense" model, developed in part based on Millward Brown research, also focuses on sensory experiences.

Chattopadhyay and Laborie (2005) have developed a tool for managing brand experience contact points. The tool allows mangers, first, to identify and select the most critical experience touchpoints, then to integrate across these touchpoints and, finally, to deliver a brand experience through cost-effective contact points. Similarly, Meyer and Schwager (2007) have presented a framework for systematically monitoring and improving the customer experience.

# 6

## Research on Online and Virtual Experiences

A large body of experience research and most frameworks have been developed for traditional, well-established experience objects (products or brands) and in consumption contexts involving services. In today's technology-driven world, however, a whole range of new media touchpoints are evolving and creating consumer experiences. Understanding interactions with, and consumption of, these media is of critical importance. Here, I will briefly provide examples of such evolving research, conducted using both modeling and interpretive approaches. The studies focus, in particular, on the internet browsing experience and social networking.

## 6.1 Internet Experience

Creating a compelling online experience is critical for gaining competitive advantage on the Internet. At least, that's been the assumption since the internet has become a pervasive information and communication medium. Both industry luminaries such as Jeff Bezos, founder of Amazon.com, and internet research firms, such as Forrester Research, have repeatedly made statements and issued popular reports that stress the importance of the online user experience. Yet, little is known about the factors that make a web site an attractive experience for users.

Novak et al. (2000) presented one of the first, and most often cited articles to address this topic. They used a structural modeling approach to measure the customer experience in online environments. At the center of their model is the "flow" construct. They conceptualize flow as a cognitive state experienced during internet navigation where the consumer is entirely focused on the activity and tunes out any thoughts not relevant to navigation. Flow, in this context, can thus be characterized by high levels of skill and control, a high level of challenge and arousal, and focused attention, all of which can be enhanced by interactivity. Similar to the experiences of flow described in other contexts, browsers lose their sense of time and self-consciousness, and they experience flow as a gratifying state.

The empirical model the authors constructed and validated on a large-sample, Web-based consumer survey, provided additional insight into direct and indirect influences of flow. For example, based on the result that challenge was positively related to focused attention (the more the web provided a challenge and stretched a user's capabilities, the more deeply engrossed and fully concentrated the user became), the authors recommended to managers that web site designs provide some challenges that get people excited so that they stay logged on, but not so many that consumers become frustrated when navigating through the site. They also showed empirical relationships to online shopping. Easy ordering, easy contact, easy cancellations, easy payment, easy returns, quick delivery, and, above all, customer support, emerged as key criteria of a compelling online shopping experience.

Mathwick and Rigdon (2004) also studied the online flow experience. They showed that flow is a critical link to transform an ordinary online information search into what they call "play," a highly positive experience that provides experiential value to the consumer. Similar to Novak et al. (2000), they found that three factors affect the quality of the experience: navigational challenge, skills to deal with them and the consumer's perceived control.

## 6.2 Social Networking

New media experiences have been examined not only from a modeling perspective but also from an interpretive, consumer-culture perspective. Consumer culture researchers have examined new online platforms — such as social networking sites (e.g., Facebook), online brand communities, video sites such as YouTube, and virtual worlds such as Second Life — to examine how consumers use these sites to relate to, reinforce, contribute to and shape contemporary consumer culture. In addition to existing interpretive methodologies, new methods such as online ethnography (referred to as "netnography") have been employed in this research (Kozinets, 2002).

Darmody and Kedzior (2009) have identified four pertinent themes based on the existing literature. First, online environments present a stage for identity construction and identity play where consumers use brands to represent their own selves online (Schau and Gilly, 2003). Second, experiences online are often tied to non-physical consumption and virtual products and services, leading to a growing dematerialization of objects and commodities (Slater, 1997). Third, relationships among consumers are growing, facilitated by the fast increase of user-generated content; as consumers interact in their own networks, their relationship to brands changes (Cova and Stefano, 2006; Muniz and O'Guinn, 2011). Finally, the social landscape of consumers is changing as a result of social networking sites and the intersection of offline and online reality; this changes consumer self presentations, impression management, friendship formation and relationship management.

Extending beyond the internet, another postmodern consumer practice is the increased consumption of reality television. Rose and Wood (2005) have used reality television as a way to study consumers' quest for the experience of authenticity. Authenticity has been presented as a frequently desired experience given the prevalence of inauthenticity — the sense of meaninglessness and superficiality in modern society (Firat and Venkatesh, 1995). Rose and Wood (2005) show, using the reality television context, that consumers must negotiate and reconcile paradoxes of identification (beautiful people vs. "people like me"), situation (common goals vs. uncommon surroundings) and production (unscripted vs. necessary manipulation) to arrive at an experience of authenticity. The programming itself does not lead to authenticity; rather, it creates "utopian places where the viewer can engage in creative play space" (p. 295). This leads to the important insight that experiences and experiential value can be, at times, extremely subjective and constructed when consumers "accept as authentic the fantasy that they coproduce" (p. 295).

# 7

---

# Experience and Happiness

---

What makes people, and consumers, happy?

Conceptually, the happiness construct is closely tied to the concept of experience. Both constructs are concerned with elements that are highly internal and subjective and are highly nonutilitarian: The experience construct transcends functional product and brand features, and benefits and quality/price relations, that lead to utilitarian value. The happiness construct focuses on broader aspirations in life, stressing, according to Seligman and Csikszentmihalyi (2000), well-being, hope, optimism, and love.

Can companies, through experience marketing, thus contribute to consumer happiness?

Addressing this question and exploring the relationship between experience and happiness is, in my view, the next step of experience marketing research.

## 7.1 Absolute and Relative Happiness

Is happiness absolute or relative? Proponents of the absolute view argue that absolute wealth and the absolute acquisition and consumption of goods matters. To put it simply, if you have more money, which allows you to acquire and consume more goods, you are happier than somebody who has less money. The relative view, in contrast, holds that happiness depends on wealth, acquisition, and consumption levels relative to others. Which view is right? As often, despite extensive research, the results are mixed.

In an article titled "Wealth, Warmth and Well-Being: Whether Happiness is Relative or Absolute Depends on Whether It is About Money, Acquisition, or Consumption," Hsee et al. (2009) provide an answer that seems to sort out these seemingly incomparable views. And the answer is within the title: it depends on whether we are measuring wealth, or the acquisition or consumption of goods. More specifically, monetary happiness, and happiness with the acquisition of a good, depends on the relative amount of money a person has; consumption happiness, however, depends on the absolute desirability of the good.

Here is how the idea was tested. Students in China were assigned to a nominal "poor group" and a "rich group" and received coupons that they could exchange for milk powder. In the nominal "poor group," some group members got one point (which could be exchanged for one teaspoon of milk powder) and others got two points (which could be exchanged for two teaspoons of milk powder). In the nominal "rich group," they received five points (for five teaspoons) or ten points (for ten teaspoons), respectively. The consumption levels (the number of teaspoons) were conspicuously marked on each cup so that everyone could see them. Monetary experience (i.e., when the groups had only their points and had yet to exchange them for powder) fits the relative pattern: the richer members in each group were happier than the poorer members in each group, but neither group was significantly happier than the other. In contrast, the consumption experience fit the absolute pattern: the richer members in each group were again happier than the poorer members, but the members in the nominal "rich group" were also happier than the members in the "poor group." Water with more milk powder just tastes better and makes you happier. When consumers drank milk, their value judgments relied on their internal sensory experiences. Thus, the utility of an item — and true happiness — lies primarily in an item's consumption utility.

However, the consumption experience does not always follow the absolute pattern. It does so for Type A variables — defined by Hsee and his co-researchers as inherently evaluable variables for which individuals have an "innate scale," including, according to the authors, temperature, sleep, boredom and orgasms (*yes*, orgasms). But the absolute pattern does not hold for Type B variables — defined as inevaluable variables for which there is no innate scale such as jewelry, handbags and cars. To support their theory, Hsee et al. (2009) conducted a large-scale field survey in the 31 officially-dedicated, main cities in China. They surveyed these city dwellers about their happiness with their room temperature and their jewelry value.

Each variable (room temperature and jewelry) entailed within-city and between-city variations. The study was also conducted in the winter: so some participants ("the rich") could afford warmer room temperatures than others. (Reported room temperatures overall varied from roughly 13.5 degrees Celsius to 21 degrees Celsius — or from 56 to 70 degrees Fahrenheit — and thus from brrrrrrrrr! to comfortable.) A comparison of the scatter plots of the relation between room temperature and happiness, and jewelry value and happiness, revealed compelling evidence for the researchers' theory: happiness with temperature was absolute but happiness with jewelry was relative. Being warm makes you happier, period. More jewelry makes you happier only if you have more than your neighbors (or reference group).

Type B variables are, of course, the type of variables that interest marketers. Type A variables (temperature, sleep, boredom, and orgasms) are something for government policy-makers, and maybe therapists. Marketers, are concerned with how they can make people happy when they market the weight of a diamond, the brand of a handbag, and the horsepower of a car. In our context, that means, how can they use experiences to make customers if not happy, then perhaps *happier*?

Perhaps we should try to understand happiness a bit better. Not so much in terms of the object of happiness (money, purchase, consumption or temperature vs. jewelry), as Hsee et al. (2009) have done, but in terms of the inherent qualities of happiness.

## 7.2   Experience, Happiness and Quality of Life

Over the last few years, there has been strong interest in happiness in the field of psychology, fostered by the emergence of the "positive psychology" movement. Regarded by Seligman and Csikszentmihalyi (2000), two of its key proponents, as a science of positive subjective experience, positive traits and positive institutions, the field of positive psychology provides an alternative perspective to psychology's decade-long obsession with damage repair and healing.

Positive psychologists have distinguished two distinct approaches toward achieving happiness: pleasure (Kahneman et al., 1999) and meaning (Waterman, 1993). The hedonic approach, dating back to Greek philosopher Epicurus, focuses on pleasure and positive emotions, and stresses that happiness results from experiencing sensorily and affectively pleasurable moments or episodes. The eudaimonic approach, first associated with Aristotle, however, focuses on meaning and stresses that happiness results from living a meaningful life and engaging in meaningful activities. That is, whereas the hedonic route concerns the small, pleasurable elements in life, the eudaimonic route to happiness focuses on a search for lasting meaning. The latter route is closely tied to so-called "terminal" values (e.g., harmony, equality, family, concern for the environment).

To examine the relation between experience, happiness and quality of life, Zarantonello et al. (2011) conducted a diary field experiment. The diary research technique (Alaszewski, 2006) seems particularly suitable for understanding individual experiences that extend over time. Following (Bolger et al., 2003, pp. 579–580) diaries "capture the particulars of experience in a way that is not possible using traditional designs"; they are self-report instruments that are useful in order to "examine ongoing experiences" and "offer the opportunity to investigate social, psychological, and physiological processes, within everyday situations."

On Day 0 (before the actual diary started) and on Day 8 (the day after the actual diary was finished) participants were asked to rate an 18-item happiness scale developed by Peterson et al. (2005). From Day 1 through Day 7, at the end of each day, participants were asked to report how much they engaged in five activities (i.e., "Eating or preparing food," "Entertaining yourself," "Engaging in physical activities," "Grooming and dressing," and "Shopping") and the degree to which each of these activities stimulated the experience type on which their diary was focused (sensory, emotional, intellectual or behavioral). Finally, each day, participants identified one activity that they had done the most and rated their happiness and perceived quality of life (Diener et al., 1985).

Results revealed that people were very happy when they focused consciously on their consumption experiences at the end of each day. This finding is consistent with the insights of positive psychology: pleasurable things and activities can make us happy, even the little things (the delicious taste of a fruit juice, the little unexpected gift at the cosmetics counter, the smile of a service employee), especially if we make a point of putting them in a meaningful context by remembering them and consciously focusing on them again, for example, at the end of a day (Ben-Shahar, 2007).

The researchers also considered the five activities in which participants engaged ("Eating or preparing food," "Entertaining yourself," "Engaging in physical activities," "Grooming and dressing," and "Shopping"). They computed the degree to which each activity stimulated a specific experience. Then they performed several correlation analyses with happiness, its sub-dimensions and quality of life. Experience level was significantly correlated with happiness and, importantly, perceived quality of life.

Finally, they checked the correlation between the five activities and, respectively, happiness and perceived quality of life. The analysis showed that all the activities contribute positively to happiness. Interestingly, entertainment is very important for life quality, whereas buying goods is the least important for both happiness and life quality. The result is consistent with psychological findings that people prefer "being" to "having" and that time rather than money contributes to happiness (Van Boven and Gilovich, 2003; Mogilner, 2010). Should we perhaps build more theme parks than shopping centers? Or perhaps different kind of shopping centers, for example, those that allow for entertainment opportunities as part of shopping sprees?

# 8

---

## Conclusion

---

As I have shown in this monograph, experiences have been researched in various fields and from various perspectives. Research has demonstrated the importance of experience in various settings (e.g., stores, events and in online and social media environments). Research has resulted in consumer insight on how consumers perceive extended experiences, how they remember experiences, whether positive and negative experiences can co-exist, how experiential attributes are processed, and whether experiences are rational. Valuable practical frameworks have been developed for managing experiences at various customer touchpoints.

Yet, the exciting field of experience marketing is still emerging. More research is needed on how experiential cues at various touchpoints create consumer experiences, and how these experiences can impact consumer behavior in the short and in the long term. We also need to study more how environments and cultural contexts can shape experiences. Most importantly, I feel we must better understand the relation between experience and happiness so that marketing practitioners — and public policy makers — provide not only utilitarian value to their customers and citizens, but also improve their well-being and life quality.

# Acknowledgments

The author would greatly thank Matthew Quint for his work and excellent suggestions.

# References

Aaker, D. (1996), *Building Strong Brands*. New York, NY: The Free Press.

Aaker, J., K. D. Vohs, and C. Mogilner (2010), 'Nonprofits are seen as warm and for-profits as competent: Firm stereotypes matter'. *The Journal of Consumer Research* **37**(2), 224–237.

Aaker, J. L. (1997), 'Dimension of brand personality'. *Journal of Marketing Research* **34**(3), 347–356.

Alaszewski, A. (2006), *Using Diaries for Social Research*. London: Sage.

Andrade, E. B. and J. B. Cohen (2007), 'On the consumption of negative feelings'. *Journal of Consumer Research* **34**.

Ariely, D. and Z. Carmon (2000), 'Gestalt characteristics of experiences: The defining features of summarized events'. *Journal of Behavioral Decision Making* **13**, 191–201.

Arnould, E. J. and L. L. Price (1993), 'River magic: Extraordinary experience and the extended service encounter'. *Journal of Consumer Research* **20**, 24–45.

Babin, B. J. and J. S. Attaway (2000), 'Atmospheric affect as a tool for creating value and gaining share of customer'. *Journal of Business Research* **49**, 91–99.

Babin, B. J., W. Darden, and M. Griffin (1994), 'Work and/or fun: Measuring hedonic and utilitarian shopping value'. *Journal of Consumer Research* **20**, 644–656.

Backstrom, K. and U. Johansson (2006), 'Creating and consuming experiences in retail store environments: Comparing retailer and consumer perspectives'. *Journal of Retailing and Consumer Services* **13**, 417–430.

Barsalou, L. (1999), 'Perceptual symbol systems'. *The Behavioral and Brain Sciences* **22**, 577–660.

Belk, R. W., M. Wallendorf, and J. F. Sherry Jr (1989), 'The sacred and the profane: Theodicy on the Odyssey'. *Journal of Consumer Research* **16**, 1–38.

Bellizzi, J. A., A. E. Crowley, and R. W. Hasty (1983), 'The effects of color in store design'. *Journal of Retailing* **59**(1), 21–43.

Bellizzi, J. A. and R. E. Hite (1992), 'Environmental color, consumer feelings, and purchase likelihood'. *Psychology and Marketing* **9**(5), 347–363.

Ben-Shahar, T. (2007), *Happier: Learn the Secrets to Daily Joy and Lasting Fulfillment.* New York, NY: McGraw-Hill.

Berry, L. (1999), *Discovering the Soul of Service.* New York, NY: The Free Press.

Bitner, M. J. (1992), 'The impact of physical surroundings on customers and employees'. *The Journal of Marketing* **56**, 57–71.

Bolger, N., A. Davis, and E. Rafaeli (2003), 'Diary methods: Capturing life as it is lived'. *Annual Review of Psychology* **54**, 579–616.

Brakus, J. J., B. H. Schmitt, and L. Zarantonello (2009), 'Brand experience: What is it? How is it measured? Does it affect loyalty?'. *Journal of Marketing* **73**, 52–68.

Brakus, J. J., B. H. Schmitt, and S. Zhang (2008), 'Experiential attributes and consumer judgments'. In: B. H. Schmitt and D. Rogers (eds.): *Handbook on Brand and Experience Management.* Northampton, MA: Edward Elgar.

Brentano, F. (1973, originally published in 1874), *Psychology from an Empirical Standpoint.* London: Routledge and Kegan Paul.

Broniarczyk, S. M. and J. W. Alba (1994), 'The role of consumers' intuitions in inference making'. *Journal of Consumer Research* **21**, 393–407.

Brown, C. L. and G. S. Carpenter (2000), 'Why is the trivial important? A reasons-based account for the effects of trivial attributes on choice'. *Journal of Consumer Research* **26**, 372–385.

Carbone, L. and S. Haeckel (1994), 'Engineering customer experiences'. *Marketing Management* **3**, 8–19.

Carbone, L. P. (2004), *Clued in: How to Keep Customers Coming Back Again and Again.* New York, NY: Prentice Hall.

Carpenter, G. S., R. Glazer, and K. Nakamoto (1994), 'Meaningful brands from meaningless differentiation: The dependence on irrelevant attributes'. *Journal of Marketing Research* **31**, 339–350.

Caru, A. and B. Cova (2003), 'Revisiting consumption experience: A more humble but complete view of the concept'. *Sage Publications* **3**(2), 267–286.

Chattopadhyay, A. and J. Laborie (2005), 'Managing brand experience: The market contact audit'. *Journal of Advertising Research* **45**(1), 9–16.

Chernev, A. (2001), 'The impact of common features on consumer preferences: A case of confirmatory reasoning'. *Journal of Consumer Research* **27**, 475–488.

Cova, B. and P. Stefano (2006), 'Brand community of convenience products: New forms of customer empowerment-the case "myNutella The Community"'. *European Journal of Marketing* **40**(9/10), 1087–1105.

Csikszentmihalyi, M. (1990), *Flow: The Psychology of Optimal Experience.* New York, NY: Harper and Row.

Darmody, A. and R. Kedzior (2009), 'Production and reproduction of consumer culture in virtual communities'. *Advances in Consumer Research* **36**, 20–26.

Davis, S. and T. Longoria (2003), 'Harmonizing your touch points'. *Brand Packaging Magazine,* (January/February).

Degeratu, A. M., A. Rangaswamy, and J. Wu (2000), 'Consumer choice behavior in online and traditional supermarkets: The effects of brand name, price, and other search attributes'. *International Journal of Research in Marketing* **17**(1), 55–78.

Denzin, N. K. (1992), *Symbolic Interactionism and Cultural Studies: The Politics of Interpretation.* Cambridge, MA: Blackwell Publishers.

Dewey, J. (1925), *Experience and Nature.* New York, NY: Dover.

Diener, R., R. A. Emmons, R. J. Larsen, and S. Griffin (1985), 'The satisfaction with life scale'. *Journal of Personality Assessment* **49**(1), 71–75.

Dubé, L. and J. L. LeBel (2003), 'The content and structure of laypeople's concept of pleasure'. *Cognition and Emotion* **17**(3), 263–296.

Edell, J. A. and R. Staelin (1983), 'The information processing of pictures in print advertisements'. *Journal of Consumer Research* **10**, 45–60.

Firat, A. F. and A. Venkatesh (1995), 'Liberatory postmodernism and the reenchantment of consumption'. *Journal of Consumer Research* **22**, 239–267.

Fischer, G. W., Z. Carmon, D. Ariely, and G. Zauberman (1999), 'Goal-based construction of preference: Task goals and the prominence effect'. *Management Science* **45**, 1057–1075.

Fishbein, M. and I. Ajzen (1975), *Belief, Attitude, Intention, and Behavior. An Introduction to Theory and Research*. Reading, MA: Addison-Wesley.

Fredrickson, B. L. and D. Kahneman (1993), 'Duration neglect in retrospective evaluations of affective episodes'. *Journal of Personality and Social Psychology* **65**, 45–55.

Frow, P. and A. Payne (2007), 'Towards the 'Perfect' customer experience'. *Brand Management* **15**(2), 89–101.

Gentile, C., N. Spiller, and G. Noci (2007), 'How to sustain the customer experience: An overview of experience components that co-create value with the customer'. *European Management Journal* **25**(5), 395–410.

Gilovich, T., D. Griffin, and D. Kahneman (2002), *Heuristics and Biases: The Psychology of Intuitive Judgment*. Cambridge, UK: Cambridge University Press.

Gorn, G. J., A. Chattopadhyay, T. Yi, and D. W. Dahl (1997), 'Effects of color as an executional cue in advertising: They are in the shade'. *Management Science* **43**, 1387–1400.

Gove, P. B. (ed.) (1976), *Webster's Third New International Dictionary*. Massachusettes, MA: G. & C. Merriam Company.

Grunert, K. G. (1996), 'Automatic and strategic processes in advertising effects'. *Journal of Marketing* **60**, 88–101.

Henderson, P. W. and J. A. Cote (1998), 'Guidelines for selecting or modifying logos'. *The Journal of Marketing* **62**(2), 14–30.

Henderson, P. W., J. A. Cote, S. M. Leong, and B. Schmitt (2003), 'Building strong brands in Asia: Selecting the visual components of image to maximize brand strength'. *International Journal of Research in Marketing* **20**(4), 297–313.

Henderson, P. W., J. L. Giese, and J. A. Cote (2004), 'Impression management using typeface design'. *The Journal of Marketing* **68**(4), 60–72.

Heska, L. (2009), *Enhancing the Employee Experience: Organizational Practices that Contribute to Employee Engagement.* VDM Verlag.

Hoch, S. J. (2002), 'Product experience is seductive'. *The Journal of Consumer Research* **29**(3), 448–454.

Holbrook, M. (1999), 'Introduction to consumer value'. In: M. Holbrook (ed.): *Consumer Value: A Framework for Analysis and Research.* New York, NY: Routledge, pp. 1–28.

Holbrook, M. B. and E. C. Hirschman (1982), 'The experiential aspects of consumption: Consumer fantasies, feelings, and fun'. *Journal of Consumer Research* **9**, 132–140.

Houston, M. J., T. L. Childers, and S. E. Heckler (1987), 'Picture-word consistency and the elaborative processing of advertisements'. *Journal of Marketing Research* **24**, 359–369.

Howard, J. and N. J. Sheth (1969), *Theory of Buyer Behavior.* John Wiley & Sons.

Hsee, C. K., Y. Yang, N. Li, and L. Shen (2009), 'Wealth, warmth, and well-being: Whether happiness is relative or absolute depends on whether it is about money, acquisition, or consumption'. *Journal of Marketing Research* **46**, 396–409.

Husserl, E. (1931), *Ideas: General Introduction to a Pure Phenomenology.* London: Allen and Unwin.

Janiszewski, C. (2009), 'The consumer experience'. Association for Consumer Research 2009 Presidential Address.

Johar, G., J. Sengupta, and J. Aaker (2005), 'Two roads to updating brand personality impressions: Trait vs. evaluative inferencing'. *Journal of Marketing Research* **42**, 458–469.

Kahneman, D., E. Diener, and N. Schwarz (1999), *Well-being: The Foundations of Hedonic Psychology*. New York, NY: Sage.

Kambhammettu, S. S. (ed.) (2005), *Customer Experience Management: Concepts and Applications*. Hyderabad, India: Le Magnus University Press.

Kant, I. (1848, originally published 1781), *Critick of Pure Reason*. London: William Pickering.

Keller, K. (1993), 'Conceptualizing, measuring, and managing customer-based brand equity'. *Journal of Marketing* **57**(1), 1–22.

Keller, K. (2003), 'Brand synthesis: The multidimensionality of brand knowledge'. *The Journal of Consumer Research* **29**(4), 595–600.

Kelley, C. M. and L. L. Jacoby (1998), 'Subjective reports and process dissociation: Fluency, knowing, and feeling'. *Acta Psychologica* **98**, 127–140.

Kingman-Brundage, J. (1989), 'The ABC's of service system blueprinting'. In: M. J. Bitner and L. A. Crosby (eds.): *Designing a Winning Service Strategy, American Marketing Association Proceedings Series*, vol. 30–33. Chicago, IL: American Marketing association.

Kishka, J. (2003), 'How to manage the customer experience'. *Customer Management Magazine* (July/August).

Kozinets, R. V. (2002), 'The field behind the screen: Using netnography for marketing research in online communities'. *Journal of Marketing Research* **39**, 61–72.

Labovitz, G. and V. Rosansky (1997), *The Power of Alignment: How Great Companies Stay Centered and Accomplish Extraordinary Things*. Wiley.

Lasalle, D. and T. A. Britton (2002), *Priceless: Turning Ordinary Products into Extraordinary Experiences*. Boston: Harvard Business School Press.

Lee, L., O. Amir, and D. Ariely (2009), 'In search of homo economicus: Cognitive noise and the roll of emotion in preference consistency'. *Journal of Consumer Research* **36**, 173–187.

Lemke, F., M. Clarke, and H. Wilson (2010), 'Customer experience quality: An exploration in business and consumer contexts using repertory grid technique'. *Journal of the Academy of Marketing Science*, published online September 2010.

Lindstrom, M. (2005), *Brand Sense: Build Powerful Brands through Touch, Taste, Smell, Sight, and Sound.* Simon & Schuster.

Loeffler, T. (2004), 'A photo elicitation study of the meanings of outdoor adventure experiences'. *Journal of Leisure Research* **36**(4), 536–557.

MacInnis, D. J. and V. S. Folkes (2010), 'The disciplinary status of consumer behavior: A sociology of science perspective on key controversies'. *Journal of Consumer Research* **36**(6), 899–914.

Mathwick, C., N. K. Malhotra, and E. Rigdon (2002), 'The effect of dynamic retail experience on experiential perceptions of value: An internet and catalog comparison'. *Journal of Retailing* **78**, 51–60.

Mathwick, C. and E. Rigdon (2004), 'Play, flow, and the online search experience'. *Journal of Consumer Research* **31**, 324–332.

Meyer, C. and A. Schwager (2007), 'Understanding customer experience'. *Harvard Business Review* (February).

Meyers-Levy, J. and L. A. Peracchio (1995), 'How the use of color in advertising affects attitudes: The influence of processing motivation and cognitive demands'. *Journal of Consumer Research* **22**, 121–138.

Mogilner, C. (2010), 'The pursuit of happiness: Time, money and social connection'. *Psychological Science* **21**(9), 1348–1354.

Muniz Jr., A. M. and T. C. O'Guinn (2011), 'Brand community'. *Journal of Consumer Research* **27**(4), 412–432.

Murphy, S. T. and R. B. Zajonc (1993), 'Affect, cognition and awareness: Affective priming with optimal and suboptimal stimulus exposures'. *Journal of Personality and Social Psychology* **64**(5), 723–739.

Nelson, L. D. and T. Meyvis (2008), 'Interrupted consumption: Disrupting adaptation to hedonic experiences'. *Journal of Marketing Research* **45**, 654–664.

Novak, T. P., D. L. Hoffman, and Y. Yung (2000), 'Measuring the customer experience in online environments: A structural modeling approach'. *Marketing Science* **19**(1), 22–42.

Oliver, R. L., R. T. Rust, and S. Varki (1997), 'Customer delight: Foundations, findings, and managerial insight'. *Journal of Retailing* **73**(3), 311–336.

Orth, U. R. and K. Malkewitz (2008), 'Holistic package design and consumer brand impressions'. *Journal of Marketing* **72**(3), 64–81.

Park, C. W. and D. J. MacInnis (2006), 'What's in and what's out: Questions over the boundaries of the attitude construct'. *Journal of Consumer Research* **33**(1), 16–18.

Park, C. W., D. J. MacInnis, J. Priester, A. Eisingerich, and D. Iacobucci (2010), 'Brand attachment and brand attitude strength: Conceptual and empirical differentiation of two critical brand equity drivers'. *Journal of Marketing* **74**(6), 1–17.

Pham, M. T. (2004), 'The logic of feeling'. *Journal of Consumer Psychology* **14**(4), 360–369.

Pham, M. T. (2007), 'Emotion and rationality: A critical review and interpretation of empirical evidence'. *Review of General Psychology* **11**(2), 155–178.

Pham, M. T., J. B. Cohen, J. Pracejus, and D. G. Hughes (2001), 'Affect monitoring and the primacy of feelings in judgment'. *Journal of Consumer Research* **28**, 167–188.

Pham, M. T., L. Lee, and A. T. Stephen (2011), 'Feeling the future: The emotional oracle effect'. Working Paper.

Pine, B. J. and J. Gilmore (1998), 'Welcome to the experience economy'. *Harvard Business Review* **76**(4), 97–105.

Pine, II, B. J. and J. Gilmore (1999), *The Experience Economy: Work is Theatre and Every Business a Stage*. Cambridge, MA: Harvard Business School Press.

Privette, G. (1983), 'Peak experience, peak performance and flow: A comparative analysis of positive human experience'. *Journal of Personality and Social Psychology* **45**, 1361–1368.

Raghunathan, R. (2008), 'Some issues concerning the concept of experiential marketing'. In: B. H. Schmitt and D. L. Rogers (eds.): *Handbook on Brand and Experience Management*, vol. 132–143. Northampton, MA: Edward Elgar Publishing, Inc.

Ramanathan, S. and P. Williams (2007), 'Immediate and delayed emotional consequences of indulgence: The moderating influence of personality type on mixed emotions'. *Journal of Consumer Research* **34**.

Ratner, R. K., B. E. Kahn, and D. Kahneman (1999), 'Choosing less-preferred experiences for the sake of variety'. *The Journal of Consumer Research* **26**(1), 1–15.

Roediger, H. L. (1990), 'Implicit memory: Retention without remembering'. *American Psychologist* **45**, 1043–1056.

Rose, R. L. and S. L. Wood (2005), 'Paradox and the consumption of authenticity through reality television'. *Journal of Consumer Research* **32**.

Sawhney, M., S. Balasubramanian, and V. Krishnan (2004), 'Creating growth with services'. *MIT Sloan Management Review* **45**(winter), 34–43.

Schau, H. J. and M. C. Gilly (2003), 'We are what we post? Self-presentation in personal web space'. *Journal of Consumer Research* **30**, 385–404.

Schmitt, B. and A. Simonson (1997), *In Marketing Aesthetics: The Strategic Management of Brands, Identity, and Image*. New York, NY: The Free Press.

Schmitt, B. H. (1999), *Experiential Marketing*. New York, NY: Free Press.

Schmitt, B. H. (2003), *Customer Experience Management*. Hoboken, NJ: Wiley.

Schneider, W. and R. M. Shiffrin (1977), 'Controlled and automatic human information processing: I. detection, search, and attention'. *Psychological Review* **84**(1), 1–66.

Schouten, J. and J. H. McAlexander (1995), 'Subcultures of consumption: An ethnography of the new bikers'. *Journal of Consumer Research* **22**, 43–61.

Schouten, J. W., J. H. McAlexander, and H. F. Koening (2007). Transcendent customer.

Schwarz, N. (1990), 'Feelings as information: Information and motivational functions of affective states'. In: R. M. Sorrentino and E. T. Higgins (eds.): *Handbook of Motivation and Cognition*. New York: Guilford Press.

Seligman, M. E. P. and M. Csikszentmihalyi (2000), 'Positive psychology: An introduction'. *American Psychologist* **55**, 5–14.

Shafir, E., I. Simonson, and A. Tversky (1993), 'Reason-based choice'. *Cognition* **49**, 11–36.

Shepard, R. N. (1967), 'Recognition memory for words, sentences and pictures'. *Journal of Verbal Learning and Verbal Behavior* **6**, 156–163.

Shostack, G. L. (1987), 'Service positioning through structural change'. *Journal of Marketing* **51**, 34–43.

Simonson, I. (1989), 'Choice based on reasons: The case of attraction and compromise effects'. *Journal of Consumer Research* **16**, 158–174.

Slater, D. (1997), *Consumer Culture and Modernity*. Cambridge, UK: Polity Press & Blackwell Publishers.

Spies, K., F. Hesse, and K. Loesch (1997), 'Store atmosphere, mood, and purchasing behavior'. *International Journal of Research in Marketing* **14**(1), 1–17.

Stephen, A. T. and M. T. Pham (2008), 'On feelings as a hruristic for making offers in ultimatum negotiations'. *Psycological Science* **19**, 1051–1058.

Thomson, M., D. J. MacInnis, and C. W. Park (2005), 'The ties that bind: Measuring the strength of consumers' emotional attachments to brands'. *Journal of Consumer Psychology* **15**(1), 77–91.

Tulving, E. and D. L. Schacter (1990), 'Priming and human memory'. *Science* **247**, 301–306.

Turley, L. W. and R. E. Milliman (2000), 'Atmospheric effects on shopping behavior: A review of the experimental evidence'. *Journal of Business Research* **49**, 193–211.

Van Boven, L. and T. Gilovich (2003), 'To do or to have? That is the question'. *Journal of Personality and Social Psychology* **85**(6), 1193–1202.

Varey, C. A. and D. Kahneman (1992), 'Experiences extended across time: Evaluation of moments and episodes'. *Journal of Behavioral Decision Making* **5**, 169–185.

Verhoef, P. C., K. N. Lemonb, A. Parasuramanc, A. Roggeveend, M. Tsirosc, and L. A. Schlesingerd (2009), 'Customer experience creation: Determinants, dynamics and management strategies'. *Journal of Retailing* **85**(1), 31–41.

Veryzer, Jr., R. W. and J. W. Hutchinson (1998), 'The influence of unity and prototypicality on aesthetic responses to new product designs'. *Journal of Consumer Research* **24**, 374–394.

Voss, K. E., E. R. Spangenberg, and B. Grohmann (2003), 'Measuring the hedonic and utilitarian dimensions of consumer attititude'. *Journal of Marketing Research* **40**, 310–320.

Vriens, M. and F. Hofstede (2000), 'Linking attributes, benefits, and consumer values'. *Marketing Research* **12**, 5–10.

Waterman, A. S. (1993), 'Two conceptions of happiness: Contrasts of personal expressiveness (eudaimonia) and hedonic enjoyment'. *Journal of Personality and Social Psychology* **64**, 678–691.

Wilson, T. D., D. J. Lisle, S. D. Hodges, K. J. Klaaren, and S. J. LaFleur (1993), 'Introspecting about reasons can reduce post-choice satisfaction'. *PSPB* **19**, 331–339.

Winkielman, P., N. Schwarz, T. A. Fazendeiro, and R. Reber (2003), 'The hedonic marking of processing fluency: Implications for evaluative judgment'. In: J. Musch and K. C. Klauer (eds.): *The Psychology of Evaluation: Affective Processes in Cognition and Emotion*, vol. 189–217. Mahwah, NJ: Erlbaum.

Zaichkowsky, J. L. (1985), 'Measuring the involvement construct'. *Journal of Consumer Research* **12**(3), 341–352.

Zaltman, G. and R. Coulter (1995), 'Seeing the voice of the customer: Metaphor-based advertising research'. *Journal of Advertising Research* **35**, 35–51.

Zarantonello, L. and B. H. Schmitt (2010), 'Using the brand experience scale to profile consumers and predict consumer behavior'. *Journal of Brand Management* **17**, 532–540.

Zarantonello, L., B. H. Schmitt, and J. J. Brakus (2011), 'Consumer experience and happiness'. Working Paper.

Lightning Source UK Ltd.
Milton Keynes UK
UKOW031808070412

190312UK00004B/1/P